Rookie STAR™
Fact Finder

10 Fascinating Facts About

Toys

by Jessica Cohn

Content Consultant

Christopher Bensch, Vice President for Collections
The Strong/National Museum of Play

Reading Consultant

Jeanne M. Clidas, Ph.D.
Reading Specialist

Children's Press®
An Imprint of Scholastic Inc.

Table of Contents

INTRODUCTION .... page 4

FACT 1 **Rubik's Cube can be solved super fast** ...... page 6

FACT 2 **A Monopoly game had 2,918 players** .... page 8

FACT 3 **The first TV video game was silent** .... page 10

FACT 4 **Barbie has had more than 150 careers** .... page 12

FACT 5 **There are thousands of different Lego bricks** .... page 14

FACT 6 **School rules led to Matchbox cars** .... page 16

FACT 7

Silly Putty went into outer space .... page 18

FACT 8

Tinkertoys came from spools .... page 20

FACT 9

Slinky walked into existence .... page 22

FACT 10

Birdie juggling is a popular game .... page 24

ACTIVITY .... page 26
TIMELINE................. page 28
GLOSSARY .... page 30
INDEX .... page 31
ABOUT THE AUTHOR .... page 31
FACTS FOR NOW .... page 32

Thousands of years ago, children played with rocks and bones. Hundreds of years ago, they tied **corn husks** together to make dolls. Today, people can pick all kinds of ways to play!

Do you want to learn more fascinating facts about toys? Then read on!

5

Rubik's Cube can be solved super fast

Lucas Etter set the world record in 2015, when he was 14.

Some people are very serious about playing with this puzzle! The world record for solving it is just under five seconds. Lucas Etter solved his puzzle in 4.904 seconds in November 2015. There is a record for solving this handheld game

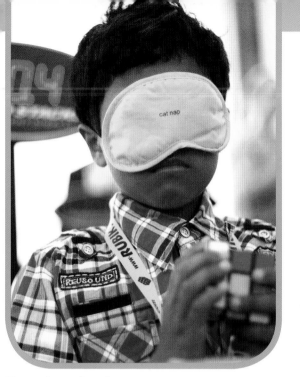

How does he do it? It is really complicated!

This popular puzzle did not start out as a toy. Erno Rubik invented it when working with small blocks and stretchy string. Rubik was studying how forms work. And when his connected blocks fell into rows, he knew he was onto to something.

while blindfolded, too! It is just over 21 seconds. Some people can even solve it using their feet!

A Monopoly game had 2,918 players

The players were not in the same room together. They did all play at the same time, though. This special game took

Darrow's game has been a top seller since 1933.

CHANCE

of Hasbro, Inc.
th dice and tokens made in China. 0009G

KENTUCKY
AVENUE

place on the Internet and at 21 spots around the world. Since the game was first released, Monopoly has been played by more than one billion people—including those who played that day!

Charles Darrow introduced Monopoly in the 1930s. At the time, the United States was going through hard times. A lot of people were very poor. With this game, everybody could play to get "rich." People loved it— and still do.

The first TV video game was silent

The first video games made to play on a TV came out in 1972. They were sold in a set called Odyssey.

The Odyssey 2001 added sound and color to the original system.

The set had games like Tennis and States, but they had no music, voices, or even beeps. What a difference from today's games!

The first computer game came out in 1962. It was called Spacewar! The makers were working on computers and they created it for themselves! Spacewar! was a game for them to play at work—it was not for sale.

Ralph Baer (below) led the team that developed the Odyssey system.

FACT 4

Barbie has had more than 150 careers

Barbie is the world's most famous fashion doll. But she is much more than just a pretty face! Barbie has held just about

Barbie's many jobs come with a lot of different outfits!

every job imaginable.
She has been a doctor, a
teacher, a race car driver—
even the president of the
United States!

Most G.I. Joe
dolls have their
nails in the
right position!

**Barbie's friend
G.I. Joe has**
lots of "looks,"
too. In the
beginning, one
nail was placed
on the wrong
side of G.I. Joe's
thumb by mistake.
And the toy's
makers left it that
way to set it apart
from fakes. People
knew they had the
real thing if their
G.I. Joe had the
odd "thumbs up."

There are thousands of different Lego bricks

The Lego company formed in the 1930s. It made wooden toys, such as dolls and blocks. In 1949, Lego started making plastic bricks. The toys had

Do you follow the instructions when you build with Legos? Or do you just look at the box?

a long name at first—
Automatic Binding Bricks.
In time, they changed the
name to Lego bricks.
Today, the company
makes 2,200 different
types of bricks.

Many Lego sets come with minifigures.

The tallest Lego tower  to date was nearly 155 feet (35 meters) tall! Children in Italy worked on it together in the summer of 2015. It took five days. The final pieces had to be lifted up by crane!

School rules led to Matchbox cars

Kids still love to play with Matchbox cars.

In 1952, little Anne Odell was preparing for show-and-tell. The teacher said that any toy brought in had to be smaller than a matchbox.

This ruled out most of Anne's toys! But it gave her dad a big idea. Jack Odell was an **engineer** who made little toy cars. He got right to work on an even smaller one. And Anne had a toy for show-and-tell!

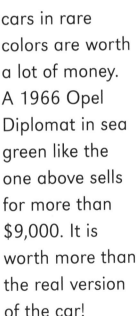

Today, Matchbox cars in rare colors are worth a lot of money. A 1966 Opel Diplomat in sea green like the one above sells for more than $9,000. It is worth more than the real version of the car!

Matchbox cars come in many different shapes and colors.

Silly Putty went
into outer space

Astronauts William A. Anders, James A. Lovell, Jr., and Frank Borman (left to right) flew around the moon.

The first people to **orbit** the moon were part of the Apollo 8 mission. Their flight launched on

December 21, 1968. The astronauts took Silly Putty on their trip. There is no gravity in outer space. Things tend to float around. The Apollo 8 team wondered how this moldable putty would act in zero gravity. They used the Silly Putty to hold their tools in place.

Silly Putty was a mistake!

James Wright came up with this simple, silly plaything while trying to make a new kind of rubber. The putty did not seem worth much— until other people saw it!

Tinkertoys came from spools

It's amazing what you can make with some circles and sticks!

Charles Pajeau started making these building toys in 1913. The idea came to him while watching kids play with empty **spools** of thread.

They kept poking sticks and pencils inside the spools. Pajeau knew the kids were onto something— especially if he added more holes.

What will these spools inspire *you* to make?

The idea for K'NEX came from recycled items, too. In 1990, Joel Glickman was at a wedding. He was playing with straws when he got the idea to make K'NEX. Since then, over 34 billion parts have been made.

Slinky walked into existence

Slinkys have changed a lot over the years.

In 1945, Richard James was looking for a way to keep objects on ships from moving around. He experimented with

springs. One day he knocked a big one off a shelf. It slinked its way down and walked over furniture to the floor. *Ta-da!* The Slinky was born!

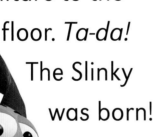

A Slinky can even be a dog! Slinky Dog was one of the stars of the *Toy Story* movies.

Slinkys are popular all around the world. In fact, if you took the wire from all the Slinkys made over 50 years, it would be too long to see. It would circle the Earth 126 times!

Birdie juggling is
a popular game

This girl is showing off her juggling skills!

The birdie is also called the shuttlecock. It looks like a cone of feathers and can be hit over a net in

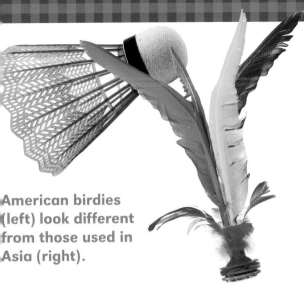

American birdies (left) look different from those used in Asia (right).

Did you know that badminton is the fastest racket sport? Shuttlecocks can travel more than 200 miles (322 kilometers) per hour! Badminton is also one of the most popular sports to play in the world.

the game of badminton. But in many parts of the world, the shuttlecock is a popular toy all by itself. In China, children pass the feather-covered toy from foot to foot for fun!

Homemade Dough

Follow the instructions below to make your own modeling dough.

You Will Need:

- ✔ 2 cups water
- ✔ a few drops of food coloring
- ✔ 2 cups flour
- ✔ 2 tablespoons vegetable oil
- ✔ 1 cup salt
- ✔ 1 tablespoon cream of tartar
- ✔ an adult to help with the stove

1 Mix all the ingredients together in a medium saucepan.

2 Ask an adult to help you place the pan on a stove over medium-high heat. Stir the mixture until it becomes thick.

3 Allow the mixture to cool.

4 Store in the refrigerator.

If you want two colors, divide this recipe in half. Use one color in each half. Or make a double batch!

Timeline

Konrad Zuse invents the Z1, the first modern computer.

The United Sates officially enters World War II.

1767 • 1936 • 1941 • 1952

A printer invents the first jigsaw puzzle, using pieces of a map.

Matchbox cars are invented.

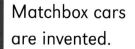

The first episode of *Star Trek* airs. The series will be turned into board and video games and launch a huge line of toys.

eBay is founded to sell collectibles, like old toys.

| 1959 | 1966 | 1972 | 1995 |

Barbie is created.

The successful arcade game Pong appears.

Glossary

corn husks (KORN-huhsks): outer coverings of corn

engineer (en-juh-NEER): someone trained to design and build complex products, machines, systems, or structures

orbit (OR-bit): travel in a circular path around something

spools (SPOOLZ): cylinders on which thread is wound

Index

1966 Opel
  Diplomat 17
astronauts 18–19
badminton 25
Baer, Ralph 11
Barbie 12–13
birdie 24–25
computer game 11
Darrow, Charles 9
dolls 12–13, 14
Etter, Lucas 6
GI Joe 13

Glickman, Joel 21
James, Richard
  22–23
K'NEX 21
Lego 14–15
Matchbox 16–17
Monopoly 8–9
Odell, Anne 16–17
Odell, Jack 17
Odyssey 10–11
Pajeau, Charles
  20–21

puzzle 6–7
Rubik, Erno 7
Rubik's Cube 6–7
shuttlecock 24–25
Silly Putty 18–19
Slinky 22–23
Spacewar! 11
spools 20–21
Tinkertoys 20–21
Wright, James 19

About the Author

Jessica Cohn has written and edited dozens of books, surrounded by toy globes, toy chairs, and other silly items. She lives in California with her family. She enjoys hiking, helping student writers, and exploring the countryside.

Facts for Now

Visit this Scholastic Web site for
more information on toys:
www.factsfornow.scholastic.com
Enter the keyword **Toys**

Library of Congress Cataloging-in-Publication Data

Names: Cohn, Jessica, author.
Title: 10 fascinating facts about toys / by Jessica Cohn.
Other titles: Ten fascinating facts about toys
Description: New York, NY : Children's Press, an Imprint of Scholastic, Inc.,
[2017] | Series: Rookie star | Includes index.
Identifiers: LCCN 2016003492| ISBN 9780531228180 (library binding) | ISBN 9780531229439 (pbk.)
Subjects: LCSH: Toys.
Classification: LCC GV1218.5 .C64 2017 | DDC 790.1/33—dc23 LC record available at http://lccn.loc.gov/2016003492

Produced by Spooky Cheetah Press
Design by Judith Christ-Lafond

© 2017 by Scholastic Inc.

Printed in China 62

SCHOLASTIC, CHILDREN'S PRESS, ROOKIE STAR™ FACT FINDER, and associated logos are trademarks and/or registered trademarks of Scholastic Inc.
1 2 3 4 5 6 7 8 9 10 R 25 24 23 22 21 20 19 18 17 16

Photographs ©: cover bear: Big Bear by arist Nathan Sawaya; cover marbles: Jesus Keller/Shutterstock, Inc.; cover rubik's cube: Boaz Yunior Wibowo/
Dreamstime; cover bus: Chris Willson/Alamy Images; cover legos: BrianAJackson/Thinkstock; 2: Jesus Keller/Shutterstock, Inc.; 3 left: Denis Gladkiy/Fotolia;
3 right: BrianAJackson/Thinkstock; 4-5 background: pialhovik/Thinkstock; 5 top: Michelle D. Bridwell/PhotoEdit; 5 bottom: nanettegrebe/Fotolia; 6: Courtesy
of David Taylor; 7 top: Rex Features via AP Images; 7 bottom left: Boaz Yunior Wibowo/Dreamstime; 8-9 bottom: CaseyMartin/Shutterstock, Inc.; 9 top:
Hasbro/Newscom; 10: Interfoto/Alamy Images; 11 top: Kenneth Lu/Flickr; 11 bottom: ayzek/Shutterstock, Inc.; 11 bottom inset: AP Images; 12: Piero Oliosi/
Newscom; 13 left: B Christopher/Alamy Images; 13 right: nanettegrebe/Fotolia; 14: Marjorie Kamys Cotera/Bob Daemmrich Photography/Alamy Images;
15 top: Piaggesi/Newscom; 15 center: esOlex/Fotolia; 15 bottom: Ekaterina_Minaeva/Shutterstock, Inc.; 16 background: Paolo De Santis/Dreamstime; 16
left: Glasshouse Images/Superstock, Inc.; 16 right: Chris Willson/Alamy Images; 17 top: ToyMart.com; 17 bottom: Tim Gainey/Alamy Images; 18: NASA; 19:
Michelle D. Bridwell/PhotoEdit; 20: Proto1138/Fotolia; 21 top: Bernard Weil/Getty Images; 21 bottom: Garsya/Shutterstock, Inc.; 22 top: Lamb/Alamy Images;
22 bottom left: Steve Weinrebe/Getty Images; 22 bottom right-23 bottom: Zuma Press, Inc./Alamy Images; 23 top Earth: Chones/Shutterstock, Inc.; 23 top
coil: photokup/Shutterstock, Inc.; 24: Luo Xiaoguang/Corbis Images; 25 left: Mikhail Olykainen/Shutterstock, Inc.; 25 top right: yocamon/Thinkstock; 25
bottom: Coprid/Fotolia; 26-27: Thomas Perkins/Dreamstime; 28 top: ullstein bild/Getty Images; 28 bottom left: British Library Board/Bridgeman Images; 28
bottom right: Chris Willson/Alamy Images; 29 left: catwalker/Shutterstock, Inc.; 29 top right: Prykhodov/Dreamstime; 29 bottom left: Chris Willson/
Alamy Images; 29 bottom right: Rauglothgor/Wikimedia; 30 top: Apples Eyes Studio/Shutterstock, Inc.; 30 center top: ullstein bild/Getty Images; 30
center bottom: Rob Gutro/NASA Goddard Space Flight Center via Flickr; 30 bottom: Garsya/Shutterstock, Inc.